SILVER COIN OF OLYMPIA

MASTERPIECES

OF

GREEK

COINAGE

49

Essay and Commentary
by
CHARLES SELTMAN

BRUNO CASSIRER · OXFORD

PRINTED IN GREAT BRITAIN
BY ROBERT MACLEHOSE AND CO. LTD., GLASGOW, W. 3
PUBLISHED 1949
BY BRUNO CASSIRER (PUBLISHERS) LTD.
31 PORTLAND ROAD, OXFORD

E   J   S

patri

in piam memoriam

filius

A   J   S

filio

magna cum spe

pater

No man is sole author of his book, least of all when it depends on fine pictures. Therefore my friends and colleagues must receive the very warmest thanks for photographs sent as well as for coins lent. They are Mr. Jean Babelon, Conservateur au Cabinet des Médailles in the *Bibliothèque Nationale*, Paris; Miss Edith Marshall in the Department of Classical Art in the *Boston Museum of Fine Arts*; Mr. John Allan, Keeper of Coins, and Mr. E. S. G. Robinson, Deputy Keeper of Coins, in the *British Museum*; Dr. H. Gebhart, Director, *Staatliche Münzsammlung*, Munich; also Captain E. G. Spencer-Churchill and Mr. R. C. Lockett who lent precious coins to be photographed, and Mr. L. Forrer and Mr. Victor Tourneur who supplied some pictures. I do not forget the various anonymous photographers who are deserving of praise. Jacqueline Chittenden has read my proofs and contributed valuable suggestions. Finally, my publisher, George Hill, is responsible for the excellent scheme of showing the same coin in its true size close to its own enlargement.

C. S.

Cambridge, 1948

Those who first see a fine Greek coin in the metal, or those who—turning the pages of a book—meet good pictures of Greek coins for the first time, are apt to enjoy a somewhat breath-taking experience, like that of men who climb the chalk Downs to find themselves on a sudden looking down on a wind-cooled sea. 'We knew', they will say, 'that the Greeks made coins; but not quite like these.'

Presently two questions perhaps are asked: When were coins invented? What sort of men made them? This essay may seek briefly to answer them.

TRADITION & EVIDENCE. Coinage was invented late in the history of mankind as a traders' device to overcome the obstacle of continuously weighing bullion, for it was the logical and practical end to a process which had begun with barter. The words of certain ancient authors, reported at second-hand by other ancient authors, support the view that this happened probably between 700 and 650 B.C. But no serious archaeologist accepts untested evidence of this hearsay kind, preferring to rely on the results of excavation and the comparative method in the study of finds from varied sites. The story about this piece of research which follows has some of the romantic quality that attaches itself so often to archaeology.

An expedition, supported by the British Museum and led by Dr. D. G. Hogarth, excavated in 1904 and 1905 the site of the once world-famed temple of Artemis at Ephesus and found clear evidence of an ancient sanctuary and basis going back before 650 B.C. Here was discovered a hoard of the oldest and most primitive-looking coins ever found, buried, as the excavators realised, under the basis for the statue of the goddess as a foundation-deposit. Together with these primitive-looking coins there were many fine carved ivories—statuettes, brooches and seals—and the excavators advanced solid arguments for dating this deposit to about the year 652 B.C. Many of the coins, having already been much in circulation before they were buried, seem to have been made a good forty years earlier.

Another most informative excavation had meanwhile been going on in Sparta, where the British School uncovered the site sacred to Artemis Orthia, and found quantities of ivory objects similar to and contemporary with those from Ephesus (*a*). The Spartan ivories in their turn were closely associated with accurately dateable pottery, and thus confirmed conclusively the arguments of those who had dug at Ephesus. Supporting evidence has come meanwhile from other Greek sites and we need not hesitate to attribute the origin of coined money to some date not far removed from 700 and well before 650 B.C. That this corresponds roughly with the hearsay evidence of certain ancient writers is interesting, and possibly fortuitous.

THE ENGRAVERS. What sort of men made these coins: or rather, made the dies from which these coins were struck? There were small beginnings.

A merchant hired a tinker to make him little punches for hall-marking bits of metal. A king of Lydia had a Treasurer who paid some occasional engraver of seal-stones to cut in metal intaglio copies of the Royal Arms so that these might be stamped on bits of gold—actually of white gold which was then the fashionable metal in Anatolia. There in the western rivers gold and silver dust was dredged up ready mixed. But this base utility attitude to coined money presently and fortunately gave place to an interest—at first benevolent, later keen, and finally passionate—in the appearance of the 'Coin of the Realm'.

There was some quality about the Greeks which induced them to endow any object in daily use with delicacy and fineness; and this same quality impelled them to create the most excellent dies that ever have been made. Not every State in Greece, but very many States, sought the services of the finest and most subtle engravers of their day to make them dies wherewith to strike money.

At this point something must be said about the attitude which the Greeks themselves had to artists, for that attitude was not entirely the same as was adopted in the renaissance and as still prevails. Many a book will talk to its readers of the *major* art of sculpture and the *minor* arts of engraving, carving and chasing. For any ancient Greek these two comparative adjectives imperatively changed places. Sculpture in stone or marble was a minor art, a craft given into the hands of artisans. Artists were the men who worked delicately in precious stones, ivory, gold, silver and bronze. They were called 'toreutai' and their

a. See Notes, p. 123.

work 'toreutiké' in Greek; and the Latin equivalents—*caelatores* and *caelatura*—come out best in English as 'celators' and 'celature' (*b*).

In the ancient world celebrated artists like Pheidias and Polykleitos acquired their fame, not as sculptors, but as celators working in gold and ivory. They did not chip marble, though they may have directed the work of artisans who did. They were famed and respected for their celature, like many of their celebrated predecessors such as Theodoros and Mnesarchos. Architects and painters were often admired for their achievements, but it was the celators whom people generally looked upon as men of the highest artistic grade, and it was from among such men that the governments of Greek States tended more and more to choose the makers of their coin-dies.

Two artists of this high quality, both of them living and flourishing about 550 B.C., deserve some closer consideration.

THEODOROS. Theodoros of Samos was a genius, and a friend of Princes who knew the worth of such men. He is credited with a number of technical inventions—the set-square, the level, the vice, the lathe, and a special method of hollow-casting bronze. His knowledge of architecture was such that he was called in as expert consultant when two of the greatest temples ever built were under construction. The work he did for famous kings called forth the admiration of that most astute and cultivated story-teller, Herodotus, who, in the fifty-first chapter of his first Book commented on a masterpiece he saw at Delphi, a silver bowl of enormous size made by Theodoros to the order of Croesus, King of Lydia, who had given it in gratitude to the shrine of Apollo. Another like it, but of solid gold, and likewise the work of Theodoros, stood in the bed-chamber of the kings of the Medes and Persians, and yet another of his magical creations was kept, men said, in the same bedchamber: a miniature grape-vine of pure gold with unripened grapes made of emeralds and ripening grapes made of rubies. But here one is on the threshhold of the Arabian Nights. There is, however, no need to regard as fanciful the story of the ring of Polycrates, told in the third Book of Herodotus, beginning at chapter forty.

Polycrates, despot of Samos, who was the principal patron of Theodoros, prospered amazingly; so much so that his timid and superstitious ally Amasis, Pharaoh of Egypt, became alarmed and wrote him a letter wherein he advised

Polycrates to avoid divine envy by casting from him the treasure he valued most and could least bear to part with. Polycrates, much impressed, considered what it would grieve him most to lose and 'made up his mind that it was a signet ring that he was wont to wear, an emerald set in gold, the workmanship of Theodoros, son of Telekles, a Samian. So he determined to throw this away, and manning a warship he went on board and bade the sailors put out to sea. When he was now a long way from the island, he took the ring from his finger and in the sight of all those who were on board, flung it into the deep. This done he returned home and gave vent to his sorrow.'

We all know what happened; how the ring was found in the belly of a fish and returned to him, and his sacrifice had been in vain. But we are not actually concerned here with the fate of Polycrates. All other considerations apart, it would seem from this story that he was a man of very fine taste, and Theodoros a very great artist.

MNESARCHOS. Another engraver living in Samos at about the same time as Theodoros was a man less celebrated for the records of his art than for being the father of his son. Mnesarchos, the engraver of seal-stones, was father of the philosopher Pythagoras; and since it was, in the sixth century B.C. and for long after, the usual custom for a son to follow his father's profession it is exceedingly likely that Pythagoras knew the whole technique of celature to perfection. From his mathematical and musical turn of mind one might suppose him to have been less disposed to value visual perception than was his father. But this is not necessarily so; and there were many aspects of the Pythagorean system which could most easily have come from the mind of a man fully acquainted both with the technique and the art of stone-engraving and die-sinking (c). At any rate, Pythagoras, son of Mnesarchos, is known to have left Samos for South Italy, where many growing Greek cities existed, and to have inspired them with his new philosophy. It is perhaps more than coincidence that those cities began at this time their first issues of coins, all of which had in shape and design a kind of Pythagorean 'twist' to them (7, 8). This will appear when you come to look at some of their coins illustrated below.

THE TRAVELS OF ARTISTS. These famous artists were much-travelled men; as, indeed, were all those Greeks who attained fame either in literature or in fine art. Of all the peoples in the ancient world the Greeks alone had an insatiable curiosity which could only be gratified by travel. The Phoenicians, of course, were especially remarkable for their voyages to distant lands; but they travelled for trade and for the pleasure of accumulating wealth. Not that a travelling Greek had any objection to making a comfortable bit out of his contacts with foreigners and other Greeks. But Herodotus remains on the whole the most typical Hellene of them all with his untrammelled desire for experience and experiment, for anecdote and history such as could only be acquired by a constant moving about the world.

Artist-celators naturally travelled about the Greek world settling for a while in any city which was enjoying prosperity. But if trouble came to that city they were among the first to leave. Having no strong civic ties, but rather a pan-Hellenic attitude of mind, being engaged in an art that could only appeal to men who were prosperous and leisured, the celators were forced to wander to some other city where work and appreciation might await them. You have but to observe a few typical cases to note the inevitability of such movements.

The subjection of western Asia Minor to the Persians in the mid-sixth century, and the consequent miseries, drove poets and artists abroad—many of them to Athens, gay with prosperity—others to seek new adventures among the Greeks of Sicily and Italy—yet others to work for the unbridled nobles of Etruria.

Soon after the Athenian victory at Marathon in 490 B.C. the fearful threat of Persian power, building up for the planned conquest of Greece, sent other artists to the West, where the threat of Carthage, though great, was then less terrifying. Yet in Athens itself the stout patriotism of Aeschylus and of many a painter and celator of Attic birth kept them at home to fight victoriously for the City. So it came about that Athens, after a brief interlude, became once more the principal centre of Hellenic art and letters. But in 431 B.C. the disastrous war against the Peloponnesians began; to be followed in the next year by the even more disastrous Plague. It was now that so many of the finest artists left to take up new careers in Sicily and Italy, to which lands the full Athenian art tradition was transferred. From about 560 to 430 B.C. the art-centre of Greece had been in Athens, and during those hundred and thirty years no other city was quite her equal.

ATHENIAN ART. In our western world today there are really two kinds of fine art. First, such art as is either of Paris or influenced in greater or lesser degree by French art. Second, there is art which is local or regional and not perceptibly influenced by Paris. The second has, scarcely ever, quite the power and liveliness and imaginative quality of the first. It was the same in the ancient world, reading Athens for Paris.

Athenian art after the victories over Persia was an international art, evidence of which you will find on the finest coins of many and widely-separated Greek cities. But alongside of this you are also going to find the production of coins that are relatively second-rate; and these are the work of local craftsmen, frequently under instruction from Athens-trained men, and having a local character in common with other local products like stone-carving and terracotta work. It must, however, be freely admitted that the work of the local die-engravers— if not quite up to that of great pan-Hellenic artists—is sometimes of very high merit indeed, for there was among the Greeks before 300 B.C. a pervading love of fineness, and this quality passed even into the common objects of everyday use.

After the year 406 B.C. it was the turn of the Greeks of Sicily to face disaster at the hands of a terrible enemy—the invading Carthaginians. Such artists as escaped massacre moved to Italy, or to Greece, now less unstable than before, and many coins of very high quality appeared in both regions. Syracuse itself, powerfully fortified and ably governed by Dionysius, still offered enough security to give employment to some fine artists; but by 350 B.C. that city had fallen so low in misery and poverty that no artist could have found employment; and, indeed, no coins were minted.

The artist by his very calling must spend his life in places where men desire his presence, and they can only want him when things are going at least tolerably well. This is what happened too in the case of those brilliant men who made the best dies for the mints of ancient Greek States.

IONIAN ART. The early coins of white gold made in Ionia (1, 2) during the seventh century B.C. mostly carry the heads or forequarters of animals, and sometimes whole animals and monsters. The work is just like that of contemporary products in gold, silver and ivory, for the coin-dies were made by the same kind of artists. When other Greek States like Aegina, off Peloponnesus (3), or Acanthus, on the Macedonian coast (4), began to coin in silver, they showed the very same power in execution, the very same sensitive knowledge of what is suited to a coin, the same understanding of how to get a signet or blazon upon something of unpredictable shape. For the coins were struck each from a die of circular shape; but the hot 'blanks' of metal, unhampered by any 'collar', assumed as they were struck forms, never perfectly circular, but rather like some irregular living organism (*d*).

From 566 B.C., when Peisistratus governed Athens, coins began gradually to have two types, and one of the types was most often the head of a goddess or a god in human guise (5). In the first stage you meet an exquisitely precise art influenced more by the draughtsman than the celator. But under Hippias, the next ruler of Athens, displaced Ionian celators found a home in the gayest city of the time, and about 520 B.C. began to make their contribution to the State's coin-dies, carving an Athene smiling and plump with an owl glossy of feather (6).

It was at this time too that another famous Ionian moved to the west—Pythagoras (7, 8). But he has already been noticed above. Some artists from Ionia moved to other parts of the Greek world. There was a wealthy city named Cyzicus on the shores of the Sea of Marmora, issuing quantities of handsome coins of white gold, and here the rich art of the Ionians continued to live on (9). It crops up too in unexpected places. Some windfall suddenly enriched a little island named Peparethus, off the Thessalian coast. In a burst of dangerous optimism, so characteristic of the Greeks, the citizens decided to have a fine coinage. A friendly and enthusiastic Ionian must have been at hand to make the dies for a lovely coin with a galloping young winged deity (10). It was a flash in the pan; but what a glorious flash!

ATHENS THE CENTRE. Meanwhile Athens was growing more and more to be the enchanted centre of Greek art. Wealth helped. It always does.

Between 490 and 480 B.C. a heavy vein of silver was struck in Attica, and the State, with no momentary call for public expenditure, decided on a share-out of extra silver among citizens. In general the ordinary coins of Athens had not often been made from fine dies like the ones mentioned above. Too many dies had been the rough work of clumsy artisans, because coin was needed in such

quantity that fine engravers—who were never abundant—could not by themselves have coped. But here was an Event, an Occasion—no income-tax, but a
handsome bonus for each citizen of ten drachmas (11), a sum with considerable
purchasing power, equal to ten weeks' pay for an unskilled labourer—say £45.
The people were agog to see the new bonus-coins and the State secured the
services of more than one accomplished engraver to make them dies.

The style employed by these engravers can be traced moving immediately after
the defeat of Persia to other Greek cities: north-easterly to Aenus in Thrace,
south-easterly to the wealthy island of Siphnos; and even to the court of a
Lycian dynast named Täththivaïbis, who combined the patronage of Greek art
with an admiration of the Cyprian Aphrodite (12 to 14, 16).

AR . . . & THE DEMARETEIA. Another man, with a background of Athenian
training close to the art of Epiktetos II and a technique rather more like a
draughtsman's than a celator's, seems to have got, about 480 B.C., to Leontini
in Sicily. There he made a pair of dies and put on one of them the letters 'A R'
—the earliest known signature on any Greek coin (*e*). But to know that his
name began with Ar . . . is about as useful as it would be to learn that there was
a fine British artist whose name began with 'Mac'. This is the more tantalising because Ar . . . transferred to Syracuse and there proceeded to make, from 479 B.C.
on, at least twenty dies for the coinage of that city, which under the able
rule of Gelon was attaining great prosperity. There had been made before this
many dies in Sicilian cities, generally—though not always—by good local men.
But Ar . . . with his new coinage associated with the name of Demarete, Queen
Consort of Gelon of Syracuse, set the very highest standard (15). The people
were enchanted with their money and there arose among many western Greek
cities a rather special civic pride in fine coinage. They longed to handle pieces
each one of which was to be a miniature work of art, and their appetite grew
with gratification. Such circumstances tended to draw celators of genius from
other parts of Greece, and mainly to attract men who had come under the
Athenian spell. Whatever city had given them birth, men knew that they could
best learn art from Athens; and even so great a designer as the Master of
Olympia drew for his Apollo on the form and concept of an Athenian model,
known nowadays as the 'Fair-haired boy'.

14

most famous coin of ancient times, indeed of all time. Evidence for its antique fame is found in many copies of the head made in those days for the coins of cities from Marseilles to Crete. Evidence for its modern popularity lies in the too frequent appearance in text books, above the caption 'Greek coin', of a photograph of one of the less successful works of Euainetos. It is strange that the large ten-drachma coins which bear his signature are the weakest of his works. But later, at a time when this great artist must have been well over fifty years old, he produced certain dies for gold coins—each coin worth a couple of silver ten-drachma pieces—and a few large silver coins marked with little griffins' heads, which proved him to the end a great master of celature (40, 41).

KIMON. It is time to turn to our third genius whom I will call, not 'the Unsurpassed', but rather 'Kimon the Unparalleled'. Many centuries later the learned Athenaeus set on record that there was a famous celator of this name (n). He must have meant the same artist who before 400 B.C. was making both gold coins and large silver ten-drachma-pieces as co-worker with Euainetos (43). The name Kimon is not confined to Athens, but is very rare elsewhere, and the probability is that our man was an Athenian who found political affairs too distressful at home and so migrated to Syracuse. He came out of the same artistic group which produced in Athens the Meidias Painter, and he did make one large Syracusan die which is almost as unpleasing in its roundness and over-tidiness as some Meidian drawing on a vase. After all, that which is wrong about Meidian art is not what it does, but how, and where. Assuming him to have been Athenian by birth, there is another guess which may fairly be made about Kimon. He could have left Athens five or ten years earlier than has been suggested and gone first to the rebel Athenian colony of Amphipolis in Macedonia, there to make silver cups and vases as well as to cut dies for some of the splendid coins with facing heads of Apollo (42). At least one of these has a real resemblance to his later signed work. He who would devise a satisfactory truncation for a facing head must include a tiny suggestion of a springing shoulder at one side or the other of the neck, and this is best achieved on some dies of Amphipolis and on one facing head which Kimon made for Syracuse. It is evident that by one pair of dies at least (44) Kimon proved himself to have a creative genius vastly beyond anything shown by any other artist of his age.

You may prefer with me an earlier art that is fresh, hard and clear cut; but you cannot fail to stand up and lift your hands in the Greek gesture of worship before Kimon's creation of the young, shining girl-goddess Arethusa with small calf-dolphins swimming through and through her perfumed hair.

And do not fail to observe that the chariot-die which he made for a reverse to this masterpiece is itself further evidence of his masterly skill.

The view has been held that work so minute and delicate as that of the finest die-sinkers must have impaired their sight after a number of years, and that no man could have made dies for more than perhaps a couple of decades. Yet one cannot positively state that no artificial aid to eyesight existed. A drop of water caught in a loop of wire is found to magnify, and a Greek would surely be quick to imitate his water-drop on a larger scale by carefully grinding and polishing a piece of rock crystal. Silence in the authors proves nothing, for they tell us no details about the art of celators. Absence of simple magnifiers in field excavations proves nothing either. An artist's lens would not be buried with him, but would pass to another. Euainetos could not have made the drachma-die—here enlarged six times—with the head of his Rivulet Boy-god (37) without a magnifier to aid him. Finally, no man devoted his whole life to the single pursuit of die-sinking. His main occupation was with vases, ornaments and armour in the precious metals and in bronze, not forgetting the delicate carving of ivory. When commissioned to make dies he might produce two or three pairs and then revert to something less tiring to the eyes. There is really no reason why a gifted man who inherited good eyesight should not work right up to the very border of old age (o).

The storm broke on Sicily in 409 B.C. with a savage Carthaginian invasion. Selinus, Himera, Akragas, Gela, Camarina, all fell before the Phoenicians. By 396 B.C. Syracuse itself was besieged; but its salvation made the turning point in the miseries of Sicily. Art was bound to retreat before this onslaught, and it was now that a movement occurred of the finer artists back towards the East. It has usually been assumed that many coins which presently began to appear in the States of Greece with heads recalling the famous coins of Euainetos and Kimon were entirely local productions. Such a view should perhaps be challenged because it presupposes that any Greek State, however small, had expert

THE COINS

———

'Owls to Athens' was the Greek proverb equivalent to 'coals to Newcastle'. The unimaginative have thought this to be an allusion to supposed flocks of feathered owlets on the acropolis. Of course it really refers to the plentiful coins in a city where every official piece bore upon its reverse an owl. Ornithologists say this is the Little Owl (*Athene noctua*) which is still common in Attica. The state seal of the city of Athens bore an owl, so here it is the bird—not the head of the goddess—which is the official coat-of-arms. And there is more to see: behind the owl a sprig of olive, generally two leaves and a fruit, sometimes a small twig: and in front three letters, *Aθε*, for *Athenaion*, 'of the Athenians'. Here are the reverse sides of the two coins last described.

5b. On the early coin of about 560 B.C., in the reign of PEISISTRATUS, is a comic little creature with gleaming eyes, almost a fledgling which might still start piping timidly for its mother. But observe the fine technique like that of a gem-engraver who has sketched

6b

5b

out all the basic design to his satisfaction. He could go on refining by adding many a dainty detail, but has decided to leave well alone. So you get an exciting effect—the strong picture of a very timid creature.

6b. The other owl, made about 516 B.C., in the reign of HIPPIAS, is a sleek-plumed, cocksure bird which no longer fears a strange world. He knows where the best mice can be had at night-time, and the best lizards after the sun is up. He has the well-bred ways of an Ionian artist and an Attic nobleman, and is equally at ease in country or in town. 'The owl's in the City' was another Greek proverb, meaning 'Jack's as good as his master'. The two coins before you are four-drachma pieces, normally the largest units of the series. There was, however, a refinement of small change, and by the end of the sixth century an Athenian citizen could have six different denominations.

7

Pythagoras, son of the gem-engraver Mnesarchos, left Samos for South Italy about 535 B.C. and re-organised the city of Croton, giving it new laws and, probably, a coinage. Pythagorean brotherhoods were formed in neighbouring cities which copied the leader's ideas. Hence the uniformity of appearance in most of their coins which bear on the reverse the same blazon as on the obverse, but in intaglio, each obverse being framed in a cable-border like that on most contemporary engraved gems. Now Pythagoras invented a doctrine called the 'duality of Opposites' involving the classification of Principles in opposing pairs: Finite-Infinite; Odd-Even; One-Many; Right-Left; Male-Female; Motionless-Restless; Straight-Curved; Light-Darkness; Good-Evil; Square-Oblong. He and his followers thought they could group every phenomenon with its opposite, and an obvious symbol of this scheme was a coin with its 'obverse and reverse',

8

its 'front and back'. Make your coin 'relief and hollow', 'positive and negative', and your symbolism is perfect.

7. The coat-of-arms of the city of METAPONTUM was a noble design originated about 530 B.C.—hardly earlier. The seven-grained ear of barley has long pearled awns and is flanked by the first four letters of the name $Μετα$. The coin is a silver stater.

8. The most westerly city whose coins conformed to this pattern was POSEIDONIA, later called Paestum, famed for its splendid temples. It took its name from Poseidon, whose statue appears upon the silver staters, and beside the figure, three letters $Ποσ$. The coin could be of about 520 B.C., and the type is not the engraver's idea of the god, but the engraver's memory-picture of the *statue* of the god as he had seen it; and that statue may already have been eighty years old when this piece was struck, hence the coin's archaic look.

9

Gem engravers of ability always stood a chance of employment in any mint which changed its main type frequently. In Asia Minor several States liked to introduce a fresh picture every year, wherein their policy was the opposite to the conservative practice in Athens which never deviated from the dignity of unchanging types. If a modern parallel be required, seek it in contemporary postage-stamp design. Britain contents itself with the Sovereign's portrait—like Athens with Athene. Most other countries miss no chance to startle or offend our eyes with new pictures. But when Greek States varied their types the desire for novelty was governed by good taste.

9. This white gold stater of CYZICUS, made about 500 B.C., carries the State's Badge, a tunny-fish, as secondary type. Most space is taken up by a kneeling Herakles holding

club, bow and two arrows. He is the signet of the annual monetary magistrate. The coin's other side is a simple punch-mark.

10. It is easy to guess why PEPARETHOS in the north Aegean Sea, a very small island famed only for its wine, should produce a burst of fine coinage around 500 B.C. The Macedonian and Thracian coast-lines passed into the Persian sphere of influence after 515 B.C., and people in Greece who had bought wine from such famous centres as Terone, Mende, Maronea and Thasos had to go without. Now, probably, Peparethus captured much of the wine-trade and for a while grew rich. The obverse of this four-drachma coin bears a large bunch of grapes; the reverse a figure of great elegance. A young god—long-haired, big wings at his shoulders, small ones at his heels, a wreath in either hand—goes flying through the air. Agon, god of the Games, or Eros, god of Love? This is the whim of a very fine engraver.

10

Marathon was fought at a time when Athens was rapidly establishing herself as the leader in art of all Greece. The patron deity of fine art was, and remained, Athene all over the Hellenic world. It is not easy for earth-bound man to think of his Holy Ones without assuming a favoured locality for them. Modern man in Bethlehem, Rome or Mecca is affected by his concepts; and you must accept the fact that once it was thus about Athene in Athens. The real religious belief of the Athenians in 'Artist Athene' or 'Athene the Worker' does explain much: not, of course, all. In 490 B.C. the Athenians defeated the Persians at Marathon. Within two or three years they had discovered in the Laureotic region of east Attica an exceptionally rich vein of silver in a state-owned mine. What to do with all this wealth? 'Give it to the citizens who own it', was the improvident answer. And so an annual bonus—this is one of the ten-drachma coins made for the purpose—was decreed. But not for long. One year 'when they were queueing for their ten drachmas Themistokles induced them to put a stop to this sharing-out, and to use the money instead for the fleet'. That is a free translation of the account left by Herodotus.

11a. Both sides of this great coin have reference to the victory at Marathon. The owl can wait. On this side it is three upright olive-leaves along the front of Athene's helmet which betoken her triumph, for they first appeared on other coins struck immediately after the victory. In style this head of the goddess is quite close to that of other contemporary Attic works of art. There is a famous marble girl dedicated by Euthydikos on the Athenian acropolis. She has a pouting expression—someone once called her 'la boudeuse' —but, were she to break into a smile, there would be a close resemblance. And in vase-painting a cup by the Brygos painter pictures a Hera with upright leaves upon her diadem and a face like the face of this Athene.

11 a

39

14 a

13 a

12 a

Formal art of an accomplished kind, strongly influenced by the formal art of Athens, is found in quite a number of states immediately after the expulsion of the Persians from Europe.

12a. Now, about 479 B.C., a flourishing Greek city in Thrace named AENUS was able to begin a coinage, and it adopted the Attic style together with the Attic monetary standard. The patron god of Aenus was Hermes, whose head in a close-fitting cap became the main design on all the coins.

13a. You can see a coin of kindred style and date from one of the islands, SIPHNOS, which long before had been peopled by Ionians from Athens. This head of the island's favourite god, 'Apollo of the Chase', has a distinct relationship to the head of Athene on the big 'bonus' coin already described. The man who made this was, however, not quite as subtle as the Hermes-head engraver at Aenus.

14a. The third silver coin, though something of a contrast, is still related. The head is that of Aphrodite, and the goddess of delight calls for a more delicate treatment than do the youthful gods. The coin was struck for the Lycian coastal city of ANTIPHELLOS by order of the local Lord, of whom more presently. But what a finished and perfectly turned-out creation is this Aphrodite. On her forehead are three rows of formal curls. Her hair is held by ribbons and caught up behind, and she wears an ear-ring of peculiar shape. Made to the order of a prince this coin shows the goddess in the guise of a lady of his court, as it were 'Sa sainteté, Madame la Princesse de Chypre'. Here is the Aphrodite of whom a Greek poet wrote that 'she stirs up sweet passion in the gods, and subdues the tribes of mortal men, and birds that fly in the air, and all the many creatures of the dry land and of the sea'.

13b

Within the square-punched, hollow reverse of a Greek coin a good engraver could do remarkable things. You have already seen owls in such a position. Now other objects present themselves as reverses to the three heads which have been described.

12b. Here is the other side of the four-drachma coin of ΑΕΝUS minted in or about 479 B.C. Hermes, whose fine head was on the obverse, carried as Herald and Divine Messenger the caduceus, or herald's staff. You note at once that the engraver who made this die

14b

12 b

knew the technique of celature, which was the same whether you thought of the god's staff as of iron, bronze, silver or gold. It is a well-balanced piece of work with a socket to fit upon a staff of oak or ebony or ivory; and the nail-heads which fastened it are shown. Αἰνιον; these are the letters of the city's name.

13b. The bird on the silver coin of SIPHNOS is a falcon, Apollo's bird (not an eagle as some have thought: other coins of other places have eagles which look quite different). This is a fine design and the letters Σιφ of the island's name help out the pattern, just as the letters did on the great Athenian coin.

14b. The pleasing object on the third coin, struck in Lycia in the city of ANTIPHELLOS, was probably a symbol of Uranus, from whom Aphrodite, often called Urania, was sprung, and the symbol passed by right to her. The strange letters set around are of the Lycian alphabet and give the name of the local Lord, Täththivaïbis, who began to rule about 480 B.C. The men who engraved these dies were all adhering to Athenian tradition, for on each coin you find the head of the city's goddess or god upon one side, and a bird or object appropriate to the same deity, set within a hollow square, upon the other. This is the Attic way of coin-making.

A R . . . , or the DEMARETEION MASTER, when he turned up in Sicily, had a task very different from that of the Athens-trained men just mentioned. He too had an Attic background, but he could not design on the Attic model because in Syracuse there already existed an old-established rule of blazonry. A four-horse chariot had from the beginning been the main coin-type, supported on the other side by a head representing the city's patron goddess—Artemis-Arethusa—with dolphins swimming round. She will be considered presently.

In 480 B.C. a Carthaginian army bent on annihilating the Greeks was heavily defeated at Himera. Stern terms were imposed on the vanquished by Gelon, king of Syracuse, and his ally, Theron of Akragas. Queen Demarete, wife of the former and sister of the latter, was alleged by later writers to have used her influence to obtain for the Carthaginians more lenient terms, and they in gratitude are said to have given her a golden crown which she promptly sold and caused the profits to be turned into silver coins. These were dubbed 'Demareteia' after the Queen, and were fifty-litra pieces—the Sicilian equivalent of an Athenian ten-drachma coin. That is the story: and most of it is clearly true, for here is one of the coins.

15a. But there was more than this one large denomination. Silver four-drachma coins with identical types were also minted; therefore it seems more correct to regard the whole coinage of the year 479 B.C. as in some special way associated with the Queen, and as a commemorative victory coinage of SYRACUSE. A four-horse chariot is moving slowly to right. A long thin charioteer stoops to touch his team with a short whip. Beneath a frightened lion streaks along; African, therefore he means Carthage discomfited. Concentrate on the near horse to see how great an artist our man is: the muscles of the neck and the folds, the hollow over the shoulder, knees, fetlocks, hooves, underbelly, what you will. The second horse is well in front of the first, the third tosses his head as Nike's wreath touches it; the fourth—a mere suggestion.

15 a

15 b

Epiktetos, the Second of that name (in former times called 'the Kleophrades painter'), was one of the more remarkable Athenian artists who lived through the period of the Persian wars. His drawing shows certain marked characteristics: full but fine lips, nostrils of unusual delicacy, almond eyes with the pupil well forward, and—often for women—smallish chins. The DEMARETEION MASTER, though a celator working not in paint but in metal, had a kindred way of doing things. There is no question of identity, but the two men are close enough in a peculiar kind of sensitivity to indicate a common tradition; and that was Athenian.

15b. The young goddess of SYRACUSE is Artemis-Arethusa, associated with a fresh spring on sea-girt Ortygia, and symbolised by a head encircled by four dolphins. They swim clockwise against a current of ten letters which proclaim this a coin 'of the Syracusans'. Now study her. The hair, parted in the middle, is waved over the temples, falls behind the ear to shoulder-level and is then caught upwards and held by a hairclip. One stray strand hangs down behind the ear. She wears as ear-ring a hoop with single drop, and a necklace of similar drops with an extra long one in front centre. She is crowned with a wreath, not of laurel, but of olive—a truly Athenian touch. The face is so delicately modelled that you are induced to imagine the bloom of her cheek. What is it in this artist's skill that makes you feel this girl has chestnut hair, golden-brown eyes and a delicate pale olive skin? All the dies of this Syracusan issue of 479 B.C. appear as likenesses of one and the same person; partly because they are all the work of one artist, but there is more than that in it; and it is now acknowledged that this date is not too early for a kind of portraiture. It is possible that this goddess has been given something of the features of Queen Demarete herself. If so, here is the best explanation why this celebrated coin was known as the *Demareteion*.

479 B.C.

Numerous cities in the northern region produced a coinage of very high quality; but none surpassed that of AENUS. You have seen its first coin (No. 12) minted about 479 B.C. just after the Persian expulsion.

16a. The second issue, perhaps of about 470 B.C., was made from dies which were even finer and more finished products than the first. There are two bronze heads in Athens—a life-size bearded warrior of about 480 B.C., and an Apollo of about 460 B.C. only half life-size. This Hermes is just half-way between the two, and is the work of an Athenian celator of genius, summoned presumably to Aenus to make dies for a city which was then exceedingly prosperous. It is the work of a mature celator with two or three decades of experience behind him. The full eye is a convention which he was loath to abandon because he had grown up with it. That it is only a convention is proved by the perfection of design and talent in execution of both sides of the coin. Aenus was in the first place a trading city situated at the southern end of the short overland route between the Black Sea and the Mediterranean. This was one reason—though not the only one—why the city's chief deity was the god most closely concerned with trade and travel. The overland route on which so much of the city's prosperity depended, had its dangers both from brigands and wild animals. Accordingly, the god of travellers was the god in whom any citizen of Aenus would most readily place his trust. That is why Hermes remained the principal coin-type for as long as the city minted money. Here he appears himself, all ready for a journey through plains and mountains. His hair, long at the back, is braided and wound tight round his head, and over it is the Pilos—a close-fitting hat of beaten felt with a slight brim; and in place of a hat-band there is a row of beads sewn to the hat.

16 a

Long before Hermes had begun an association with the market-place he had been a protector of flocks and especially of goats, so that it was natural for the goat to become his sacred animal. In Athenian art, and especially in Athenian black-figure painting, you will find a long series of superbly drawn goats, for these animals, having so great a reserve of strength in so relatively small a body, clearly had a great appeal to the Greek mind. There is something natty and nasty, fascinating and fearful about a well-groomed he-goat.

16b. That description is surely true about the first of these animals to appear on the four-drachma coins of AENUS. You would say he has been curry-combed, the clippers have been over him leaving a ridge of bristles down his spine, and his beard and forelock have been lovingly brushed. Over his back the first four letters of the city's name are engraved, and in front of him a supplementary design is placed. You see a throne shaped as a high-backed arm-chair. Over the back is hung a wreath and on the seat stands an image. It appears as an unwrought stump of pine, or some other conifer, to the top of which a head has been attached—a bearded head of the god wearing a conical cap topped by a knob, quite different from the hat worn by the god on the other side of this coin. In front of the image stands an upright caduceus which has three loops, instead of the usual two. Beyond all doubt you see here the picture of a primitive cult-image which was already very ancient when this die was made about 470 B.C.; a luck-bringer to which a traveller might give a wreath before starting on a journey, and to which he might sacrifice a he-goat after a safe return. It is evident that this primitive image was held in great veneration at Aenus, for it recurs again and again on the coinage for many years.

16 b

17 a

Hieron, a man of imagination, succeeded his brother, Gelon, as ruler of Syracuse. On the slopes of Mount Aetna lay Catana, which he caused to be re-built and re-named AETNA, and it became his absorbing hobby. He got Pindar to write him, as 'Lord of Aetna', an ode; and he got the finest engraver of the day to make him dies, both events probably in 470 B.C. The engraver had no set subject to re-create, and, since he was making dies for a brand new city, he was free to invent brand new types.

17a. So it came to pass that this man, whom we now call the AETNA MASTER, made the most magnificent head of a seilenos in all art. The eye is a profile eye, just as it is for the seilenoi in numerous Attic vase-paintings which still retain the full-eye convention for gods, heroes, and mortals. His shiny scalp, tidy hair-fringe round the back, neat moustache and beard, sharp ear and stylised ivy-wreath are all perfection. Below is one of those scarab-beetles which attained a great size on Mount Aetna. Firm, well-spaced letters tell that this is a coin 'of the Aetnaeans'.

18a. Nine years later the same artist did equally good work for another Sicilian city, NAXOS, which regained independence in 461 B.C. This time the head is of that god who is the lord and master of all seilenoi—Dionysos. There is plenty in common with the older coin: formalisation of beard and moustache, muscles of the neck; and with it all a feeling of human animal majesty. By the time the Aetna Master made this die for the four-drachma coin of Naxos he was not quite so careful, but if anything, more accomplished than when he made the die for Aetna with Seilenos. These two dies together show Athenian influence as rich and strong, for you think of painters like Epiktetos II, Makron, Duris and that Polygnotos called 'the second', all of whom loved to paint a Dionysiac rout. But you also think of Olympia, for these are pan-Hellenic masterpieces.

18 a

Compositions of two different kinds were used by the AETNA MASTER for the reverses of the coins just described; both entirely original for coins, though there are near-parallels on vases by men like Epiktetos II, Makron and Duris.

17b. Zeus, God of Mount AETNA, is seated on a fine throne which you must think to be of gold and ivory; the pelt of some dappled wild-cat is thrown over the seat. The god wears a long cloak which leaves the right arm and breast bare, and rests his hand on top of a long, twisty, walking-stick such as the gentry are seen to carry on Attic vases. In his left hand is a handsome thunderbolt. In front grows a pine-tree from the forest-clad slopes of Aetna. On the top perches the god's eagle and the tree sways slightly under its weight.

18 b

17b

18b. The other four-drachma coin made nine years later for NAXOS is a contrast. Attic painters come to mind again and so does a gem engraver named Anakles. But the Aetna Master, the Athenians and Anakles, are in one tradition because it is pan-Hellenic and because Athens is its home. Before you study the subject, note the well-placed letters of the Naxian name, cut by the same hand as the letters on the older coin. The subject: Seilenos, physically perfect, squatting facing, his right knee up, left thigh level; mane, beard, tail, like other hair by this artist. He turns toward a metal cup held in his right hand. Among many ugly and un-Greek heritages from medieval Puritanism is a habit of using 'animal' applied to man as a term of abuse, when the term should, of course, only be an unprejudiced reference to one aspect of humanity which can be just as good (or non-good) as the aspect called 'spiritual'. The point is necessary because, when the figure of this superb seilenos is called—as called it must be—magnificent in its animal vitality, this is to be understood as most high praise—never as a petulant pejorative. Magnificence of this kind is here portrayed as on no other monument.

19 a

Far to the west in Sicily, on the banks of the 'Celery River', men founded a city to which they gave the river's name, and that in Greek was Selinos. With the sole exception of Marseilles this was of all the big Greek cities the most westerly, though you would never guess from its coin types that it was in any way distant from the rest. In earlier days a simple, unimaginative pun had provided a coat-of-arms. Your city is called Celery; it is on the banks of the Celery River where a great deal of wild celery is growing. So you take a leaf of celery as your blazon. However, in or soon after 467 B.C.,

20 a

there arrived a celator with ideas who began to make for the city dies which showed much imagination—not local, but pan-Hellenic in character, for he produced dies which compare most favourably with work which contemporary masons were doing on stone panels for one of the city's temples. There were two main denominations.

19a. A four-drachma coin has a small chariot drawn by four horses; the reins are held by Artemis, and beside her stands her brother, Apollo, bow in hand, about to shoot. He recalls the Siphnian Apollo of the Chase (No. 13). The horses are not quite as good as Queen Demarete's horses (No. 15), but they do please. The goddess is not as well-defined as the god. Nevertheless, a brave attempt at a difficult composition has been made.

20a. The two-drachma coin shows a wiry, athletic Herakles clubbing the Cretan bull—a small, rather gentle bull, with a fine wrinkled neck and dewlap, which the hero seems to subject to needless violence. With his left hand he has the little steer by the right horn; with his left knee and foot he tackles its near foreleg to throw it off its balance, and you see he is about to lay it out with a blow between the eyes from his club. Both coins bear a legend with the name of the Selinuntines.

20 b

Quiet standing figures, elegant and athletic, occupy the reverse sides of the two coins made for the people of Selinos about 467 B.C. At this time Olympia and other Sanctuaries were being peopled with statues in bronze of athletes, and of gods and heroes in the guise of athletes. In the age of unreason and destruction when naked marbles were mutilated by fanatics, statues of bronze were melted down, therefore hardly any survive. But their abundance influenced artist-celators like the makers of these fine coins.

19b. The Greeks, who personified the forces of nature, were often given to representing the god of a river as a handsome youth. Here, on the four-drachma coin is young 'Celery-river' himself, a shallow silver bowl for drink or libation in his right hand, a branch of laurel in his left. There is an altar before him and a large cock. Behind him on a rectangular block is an anvil-shaped base upon which is a fine statue of a bull. In the field of the coin, over this bull, is a celery-leaf—coat-of-arms of the city of Selinos. The young god is labelled Σελινος.

20b. A smaller river, the Hypsas, was a tributary of the main stream, and so this must also have its young god, who is labelled Ηυψας, and who suits the smaller two-drachma coin. He is not unlike his elder brother, though shown more frontally; he too has a

19 b

shallow bowl and a laurel-branch, and he too has an altar before him, though here a bearded serpent coils round it. Behind a long-legged water-fowl walks away and over it again is the celery-leaf, as a blazon of the state. What precisely are these youthful gods about? Each has an altar before him and an animal; and cock and snake are both sacred to Apollo. Perhaps it is enough to say that, since a mortal man likes to have wine offered him at a feast by a handsome youth, the Olympians, Apollo and Herakles, like to receive libations of wine from the handsome young demigods of the rivers.

22

Vitality, of a kind to astonish one even now, animated all Greece for many centuries. It was apparent in many ways, and among artists of the fifth century B.C. it showed itself most clearly in a preoccupation with sparkling youth. You perceive that gods and goddesses, demigods and nymphs, all become exquisitely young. Vase-painting in Athens will be telling you the same thing; and you may shed all preconceptions about 'schools of art' in Greece. After 480 B.C. there was a Greek classical art. If it had a headquarters it was in Athens; but it appeared also in Corinth, Olympia, Lesbos, Italy and Sicily, for it was pan-Hellenic.

21. TROIZEN, in north-eastern Peloponnesus, was closely linked to Athens. Here about 460 B.C. you see a silver drachma with a head of Athene as a girl-goddess, unhelmeted, finely-modelled. An eye, still almost full, makes it difficult to be sure of the date. But there were engravers in Athens and elsewhere (Nos. 12–16) who were loath to drop the full-eye convention. This coin's reverse has the trident of Poseidon.

22. MYTILENE, capital of Lesbos, was the mint which issued a splendid stater of white gold with the head of a boy Apollo, laurel-wreathed. The Pan painter in Athens, about 450 B.C., towards the end of his career, drew some young heads that remind one of this,

22   23   21

23

but he never quite attained this excellence. Only a quartered punch-mark here for the other side.

23. Corinth had several flourishing colonies, among them one at AMBRACIA (now Arta) where about 440 B.C. a fine engraver made for a silver stater a die with the head of Athene as a young girl wearing a helmet of Corinthian shape. The little metal drinking-cup behind her head is the private signet of some moneyer. On the other side of this coin is the winged horse, Pegasus, the blazon not only of Corinth herself, but of all her loyal colonies.

21

Zeus, the Father of gods and men, was not youthful. His vitality was of another kind; of Spirit and of Mind.

24. There was an engraver whose name began with Da . . . and who worked at OLYMPIA. Fourteen years after Pheidias had there completed his world-famed gold and ivory statue of Zeus, this engraver made certain dies for coins that were issued for the great Olympic festival of 420 B.C. If he was influenced by Pheidias, that cannot be known, since no work by Pheidias survives. But it is clear that he did owe much to the influence of an older artist, the Master of Olympia, for there are heads among that artist's works which Da . . . knew very well indeed. The silver two-drachma coin is not well-preserved, and there is a disturbing counter-stamp upon the neck of this noble olive-wreathed head

24

of the god. Yet nothing can mar the divinity of its dignity. The engraver's signature is on the reverse side of the coin, low down on either side of a thunderbolt, within a wreath of wild olive.

25. The head of an eagle, bird of Zeus, is on the obverse of another silver two-drachma piece of the same year by the same artist. Under it is a leaf of white-poplar from the sacred tree which Herakles, men said, had once brought from northern lands to plant at Olympia. The reverse of the second coin is rather like that of the first. Guesses have been made about this artist who, one scholar thought, might have been a bronze-worker, Daidalos of Sicyon; while another thought he could have been Dexamenos of Chios, engraver of seal-stones. The latter guess was not a good one; the former can only be verified if an original bronze by Daidalos is ever found.

26 a

Phrygillos, whose name means 'Finch', was an engraver about whom a good deal can be learnt. A carnelian seal-stone with his signature is preserved, and the city in which his activity is first apparent was Thurii, an Athenian colony in South Italy. It was about 430 B.C. that he began to make fine dies for this city, and it is possible that he actually left Athens about then to escape the plague. His work has a very special purity which calls to mind that of certain classical Athenian painters at work between 450 and 420 B.C.; the Achilles painter, and his pupils like the Phiale painter. Three silver two-drachma pieces made for three different south Italian states, and a coin from a Sicilian city as the fourth, will introduce his style.

27a

26a. THURII: Athene is patron goddess here as in the mother-city, Athens. A fine close-fitting helmet, bound with a wreath of olive, carries a well-trimmed horsehair crest. It is worn by a young Athene who looks like the grand-daughter of the big Athene (No. 11 above) of about 487 B.C. The engraver's initial φ is in front above.

27a. You see the initial φ again on the most dainty die which Phrygillos made—this one for the city of TERINA, down south on the west coast of Italy. Here is the patron-deity, the goddess-nymph 'Nike-Terina' within a wreath of olive. Her hair is rolled up over a finely-embroidered head-band. Only on some Athenian vases with drawings by the Achilles painter can you find anything to equal the delicacy and elegance of this head. This is the work of the same man who engraved the Thurian die, and you are inclined even to think that it is a likeness of the same girl—that the same model 'sat' for both coin-dies. A dangerous assumption; it is wiser to suppose that Phrygillos had his own ideas of young female loveliness and translated them into metal for his and our delectation.

27b

Phrygillos, at work in the four cities, made the other dies also for each of the various coins.

26b. For THURII he made a die with a bull. That animal being the official coat-of-arms; over it the name Θουριων 'of the Thurians'; in the underspace a fish, and under the bull's legs a finch: this is a punning signature for the engraver himself whose name, you remember, means 'finch'. The letter φ appears on the bull's haunch just below the root of the tail. There are many other bull-dies by him, on some of which the first letters of his name, φρυ, replace the bird. Bird and fish and bull all seem to fit admirably into the pattern of this coin. The same kind of fish is going to occur on another coin in another city. As for the bull: that had been the blazon of the ancient city of Sybaris which had preceded Thurii long before.

27b. Of all his reverse dies this one cut by Phrygillos for TERINA about 425 B.C. is the best. Nike, whose left wing makes a halo for her face, sits on an overturned vase. Notice the perfect modelling of face, neck, breasts and hands. In her right a caduceus, and

26 b

perched on her left forefinger a bird; once again the sign of our 'Mr. Finch'. The name 'of the Terinaeans' is engraved in front. Bewilderment came to archaeologists in the past who tried to derive this work from that of the accomplished stone-masons who carved a parapet for the bastion of Athene-Nike in Athens. If there was any debt it was certainly the other way. The exquisite seated Nike-Terina, teasing her finch, is in feeling close to the Muse on Mount Helikon—she also has a bird near her—upon a white vase by the famous Achilles painter of Athens. In fact, the Achilles painter and Phrygillos are both of them men of that generation which may have taught the five or six carvers who worked at the parapet of the bastion of Athene-Nike in Athens.

28 a

Undeterred by commitments at Thurii and Terina, the brilliant PHRYGILLOS was ready to undertake various new commissions. He must have delighted in travel, for he seems to have moved from Thurii and Terina to Hyele and Leontini within a short space of time; then to Syracuse, and presently back to his favourite Thurii, and thence to Pandosia and Italian Heraklea. After that possibly—though here it is more of a guess— he ended his days in the eastern Greek city of Sinope.

28a. His initial, ϕ, is on a coin made about 425 B.C. for the city of HYELE, sometimes called ELEA, and famed for the philosophical school of Xenophanes, Parmenides and Zeno. The delicate girl's head is that of the fountain-nymph 'Hyele', meaning 'moist-girl'. An ancient commentator on Aristophanes tells that Dionysos was sometimes called 'Hyes' or 'moist-one'. Was the nymph one of his daughters? The grape-vine might support this view, but it remains a guess.

29 a

29a. Twenty miles to the north-west of Syracuse lay the city of LEONTINI which for a
bare half-century enjoyed independence from its too-powerful neighbour. Its main coin-
types were a lion's head and the head of Apollo; and in general local engravers with
mediocre talents made its dies, though on occasion a fine celator was called in. One such
occasion was about 424 B.C. when Phrygillos came straight, you would think, from
Hyele to make an almost perfect head of Apollo. Behind the head is an ivy tendril, like
the grape-vine tendril of the Italiote coin, and the engraver's initial φ. In the year
422 B.C. the city of Leontini became a mere dependency of Syracuse and in consequence
ceased to issue money. Accordingly, the date of this, one of the very latest of its four-
drachma pieces, can be known with some degree of accuracy. It is natural to compare
this Apollo with the famous bronze athlete's head from Beneventum of the same date.
The latter has the modest demeanour of a mortal; the die by Phrygillos represents the
audacity of a god.

29 b

The work of your very versatile artist—and PHRYGILLOS was such a one—is always the most difficult to date. One might class these coins of Velia and Leontini as earlier than the two of Thurii and Terina (Nos. 26 and 27): but the Thurians are two dies out of many which he was making there over a period of years, and his earliest Thurian dies precede any of his others. Meanwhile the coin of Leontini comes near the close of a series which had ended for good in 422 B.C., so the margin for dating is a narrow one.

28b. For HYELE he made a die with a lion: crouching, cautious, tail between legs—a timid lion. In the underspace is an owl for Athene, whose worship in Hyele is proved by later coins. The lion is leonine, and therefore the work of a man who had seen such a beast, which he could have done in the Balkan peninsula since they were common in Macedonia and Thrace. The fact that Phrygillos knew the creature's appearance may indicate that he was no South Italian by origin, for such men made lions which resembled dilapidated poodles.

28 b

29b. A contrast: this for LEONTINI is not a lion at all; only a leonine *thing*, for it is really a waterspout, such as architects put on the eaves of temple-roofs to carry off rain-water, or such as builders fitted to fountains so that fresh water gushed from a lion's mouth. A lion is 'leōn'; a lion-headed spout 'leontis', and the coin is inscribed 'Leon-tinon', which is taken to mean 'of the Leontines'. It was usual to surround the lion-spout with four grains because the city was the centre of a great corn-growing region. Occasion-ally one grain was replaced by something else; in this case, when Phrygillos made the die, by the very same fish which he had engraved upon dies at his headquarters in Thurii. The fish here points to Phrygillos as author of this die almost as clearly as does the φ behind Apollo's head on the main side.

31 a

Celebrity, won in south Italy, may have led the Syracusans to invite PHRYGILLOS. In any case by about 416 B.C. he got to Syracuse, and at least four dies which he made found favour with the State. Nearly twenty years earlier certain local men had begun to sign Syracusan coins, and very skilled celators like Eukleidas and Euainetos had joined them several years before Phrygillos arrived. In a great city much less variation was permissible than in a small one: on one side of the four-drachma coin there had to be the head of a goddess, four dolphins and the name 'of the Syracusans'. Upon the other side a four-horse chariot was obligatory. Phrygillos never attempted the latter, but the head-dies which he made were entirely charming.

30a. You have seen on Queen Demarete's coin what was expected at Syracuse, and how important dolphins were. You are going to see a die made by Euainetos (No. 35) a few years before the arrival of Phrygillos, with lively, sleek, violently muscular dolphins. But the first dolphins of Phrygillos clearly proclaim him a 'foreigner' unaccustomed to their presentation on a coin-die, for the creatures are softish and do not quite suggest a mechanism of steely muscles under an oily black hide. But the head of the goddess delights. It is individual, as though some girl had been the model. This, however, is not the usual Artemis Arethusa. In 415 B.C. Phrygillos and a local colleague, Eumenes, both made dies to go with the chariot-die by a third artist, Euthymos, but the two who made the head-dies both depicted, instead of Artemis, Persephone crowned with an ear of corn, a poppy-head and an odd leaf. The reason for the brief change to the head of this goddess escapes us. Below our man writes his name in full, *Φρυγιλλος*,

31a. On the other dies for four-drachma coins he signs *Φρυ* upon the band on the forehead of the young goddess—Artemis Arethusa once more—very like the Nike whom Phrygillos carved a few years earlier at Terina; and now he has learned how to make successful dolphins.

30 a

Racing chariots should not present too great a problem to a skilled celator, and long before this, Athenian and Corinthian painters of black-figure vases had managed them nicely. However, in SYRACUSE, from the appearance of the very first four-drachma coin down to about 435 B.C., slow-moving chariots driven by long-robed drivers, bearded or beardless, had been the rule. Then Eumenes started on dies with teams of prancing animals, and made such a mess of his design that one may think he discouraged Phrygillos from attempting the unfamiliar, and chariots for the coins with Phrygillan heads were made by others.

30b. First EUTHYMOS: a clever design of four horses trained in circus-like action, all eight front-legs raised to paw the air. No mortal, but a winged Agōn, god of the Games, drives them; and Nike flies to crown him. The under-space is abnormally large, for something special has to go in as well as $Ev\theta$ . . . , the first three letters of the artist's

30 b

76

31 b

name. You see the monster, Skylla, Guardian of the Straits, trident over her shoulder. Out of her hips grow monstrous dogs which she is egging on to attack a terrified fish, and this must allude to a reverse sustained in 415 B.C. by the Athenians at the hands of the Syracusans.

31b. EUARCHIDAS set a different goddess in the chariot; Persephone, who holds out in her right hand a flaming torch. Nike flies to crown her; an ear of corn fills the under-space. The horses in high action owe much to certain horses by Euainetos which you are going to see. This is a great *tour de force*, but it is really an uncomfortable design for one reason only—the goddess-driver is much too big. These chariot dies and others very like them link up with another contemporary work of art—a splendid silver bowl in New York of the very same style and date.

32 a

People who took as great a pride in their money as did the Syracusans could not fail to show upon their coins references to their fortunate deliverance in 413 B.C. from the Athenian menace. Large silver coins had more than sixty years before commemorated a Syracusan victory over Carthage. Once more large coins were planned, and designs by two artists were accepted, but not those made by PHRYGILLOS. The evidence that he probably submitted a design is a solitary trial-piece or proof, in lead, the head on which is in his characteristic manner. He returned to Italy about 412 B.C. to make more dies for his old patron-city, Thurii, for Pandosia, a hill-town near Terina, and for the flourishing city of Heraclea on the gulf of Tarentum. What he had learned in Sicily showed itself in several ways, since an artist learns from both colleagues and competitors. 32a. For PANDOSIA he produced a most attractive facing head of Hera, having doubtless studied the technique of celators in Sicily who sunk dies with facing heads for Catana and Camarina. After Phrygillos this facing Hera found imitators in more than one Greek-Italian city.

34a. It is possible, though by no means certain, that Phrygillos, after 406 B.C., moved to SINOPE on the southern shore of the Black Sea. If he did not go himself, then a clever pupil who reproduced the master's style went in his stead; for the head of a nymph on a silver drachma of that city closely resembles his Syracusan Artemis Arethusa, and has a great superiority over most other coins of this eastern Greek city.

34 a

33 a

33a. At HERACLEA about 410 B.C. he made a reverse die with Herakles which you see over the page. The obverse to this piece was the work of a colleague named ARISTO-XENOS, a younger man who learned from Phrygillos, and whose signature in minute letters appears on some of his dies along the base-line of the crest worn by Athene on her helmet.

34 b

Of these three reverse dies, two must be the work of the celator PHRYGILLOS, and, if the third is not also a work of the master, it is very close to him.

32b. Pan, god of the hills and valleys, is a perfect canting-type for the hill-town of PANDOSIA. He appears as a young hunter, horned, naked but for a cloak at his back, seated at ease on a rock, two short hunting-spears in his right hand; his hound lies beside him alert. Before him is a wayside terminal figure—a phallic Herm to which is affixed a caduceus with dependant fillets. Above at Pan's shoulder-level is the engraver's initial ϕ.

33b. Phrygillos made for HERACLEA a superb die with Herakles beginning to strangle the Nemean lion, which is wonderfully like the beast he made years earlier for the town of Hyele (No. 28), and which is the work of a man who knew what lions look like. The hero, who has cast aside club and bow, is tense in every muscle. The familiar initial is there between his legs. Both these male figures—Pan and Herakles—show the artist's skill and imagination to great advantage. Added to his earlier repertoire of bull, lion and seated Nike, they give a picture of his wide range.

34b. SINOPE is a long way off: but then such artists as Phrygillos were always travellers, and at the end of the fifth century B.C. the Black Sea coast was less troubled than the shores of Sicily and Italy. Phrygillos, or his clever pupil, who made this die of a sea-eagle on the back of a young dolphin, had learnt at Syracuse how to make dolphins properly. And a man who loved small birds, like finches, could well have made this excellent eagle. The letters $M\iota\kappa\alpha$ above are part of a moneyer's name, while $\Sigma\iota\nu\omega$ below is the name of the city. And here you leave this interesting artist, some of whose life it has seemed possible conjecturally to re-create.

33 b

32 b

EUAINETOS, had he been Head of the Office of Works and Director of Building in any great Greek city or sanctuary, would have been just as famous as Pheidias. Hellenistic and Roman compilers would have written him up and nineteenth-century antiquarians would have attributed to him several disagreeable marbles. Fortunately you can estimate this great artist as you estimate an Athenian vase-painter, without pedantic

35 a

preconceptions to confuse you; for you are going to see several examples of the art of Euainetos and his fellow-workers on dies made for Syracuse and some other Sicilian cities, and to examine his versatility and his almost unfailing good taste.

35a. His whole background and training was clearly Athenian. He may have got to SYRACUSE about 430 B.C., and not more than five years later he had made dies, both obverse and reverse, for four-drachma coins, that put local men into the deep shade. Take first his chariot. Here is simplicity, realism and fine composition. The bearded charioteer is an expert, and is in proper scale with his horses, which are lovely creatures.

The chariot, with its great wheels, is right—mechanically right. Yet this realism does not spoil composition, and one likes the rubber-tough dolphins of the under-space, and starts with surprise at a Nike resembling a Renaissance angel, who carries a tablet inscribed with the artist's name, *Ευαινετο*. There is something almost arrogant in the boldness of this signature.

36 a

36a. This same feature is there in another coin made about the same time for use in neighbouring CATANA; and here is the same true scale between horses, driver, and big-wheeled chariot. On the right is the winning-post, just passed, and so the driver begins to rein-in the horses in their wild energy. Below, instead of dolphins, a fresh-water crab (here subject to an unintentional double-strike) from the river Amenanos, the Spirit of which was venerated by the Catanaeans. Both these chariot-dies are unrivalled. Some others were about as good—none better.

That liking for youthfulness, which had been characteristic of Attic tradition twenty-five and more years before, was also evident in the earlier work of EUAINETOS. Yet there is a difference. The older engravers, moving about in Peloponnesus and the Islands, drew for their inspiration upon impressions of the healthy children of strong farmers,

36 *b*

sailors, and small-town gentry of good family. The models which registered in the brain of Euainetos were the sons and daughters of the very rich, very sophisticated plutocrats of Sicily. But do not fail to notice that Euainetos himself moved in those same social circles, and that is why he was so sensible about race-horses and chariots: he was intimate with the owners.

35b and 36b. The two four-drachma pieces before you, one for SYRACUSE and one for CATANA, are so very alike that you must study them together, for they are brother and sister: fountain-girl, Arethusa, at Syracuse; river-boy, Amenanos, at Catana. Little snood-scarf has every fold in place, large laurel wreath every leaf; and on one head and the other you do not see one tiny lock that is out of position. The four dolphins, obligatory for coins of Syracuse, are round her head, and if the belly of one of them in front of her lips

36 b

were not so deep in shadow, you would see there inscribed the signature *Εὐαι*. The boy Amenanos has, instead of dolphins, a fresh-water cray-fish, and, sweeping round in front of his face, a curious object. It is a woollen fillet with four wool bobbles, a loop at the top for hanging it up, and at the bottom-end a little bell. Such things were hung by votaries in temples and out-of-door shrines where a small breath of wind could set them tinkling. Lastly, observe on both the fine, compact and well-placed lettering, which tells in each case by an unbroken word that this is a coin 'of the Syracusans', or 'of the Catanaeans'.

Amenanos, the little river flowing through the city of CATANA, was thought of by EUAINETOS as a very small boy.

37. Here is a lovable, half-animal creature with the perfect skin of a healthy child, and with budding horns and downy fur that sprouts down his forehead. The hair is restrained by a triple-ribbed head-band above which, in front, rises the little horn of a river-god. Yet hair grows very low on the brow because there is a touch of pony blood somewhere; for this is the grandson of that horse-tailed seilenos whom the Aetna Master created for the people of Naxos (No. 18). The name of this fairy-child, Ἀμενανος, is inscribed above his head, and underneath, the first four letters of Euainetos' name. If none of the other coins made from dies by this man had survived—neither the pair of four-drachma pieces, nor the fifty-litra silver, nor the hundred-litra gold (Nos. 35, 36, 40, 41)—this one little silver drachma, small as a sixpence, would be enough to tell that Euainetos was an artist whom some have equalled but none surpassed. The 'frame' is made partly of letters and partly of things from the river—two bony freshwater fish and a prawn. The obverse of this tiny coin has a four-horse chariot, big-wheeled, driven by a well-designed charioteer whom Nike crowns. The name 'of the Catanaeans' fills the under-space, and the whole die is designed in the manner of the bigger pieces already described. Finally, you will not fail to note that this coin can be enlarged up to six diameters and can only gain thereby. Its date: about 420 B.C. Euainetos, who surpassed all his fellows but Kimon, was probably chief among several other celators of mark. Reference has already been made—apart from the 'foreigner' Phrygillos—to Euthymos, Euarchidas and Eukleidas, all in Syracuse. But since the Master had associations with two smaller cities, Catana and Camarina, it becomes clear that certain men who made dies for these lesser cities were also associates of his group; and they deserve attention too.

37

87

41 a

Euainetos was perhaps the most prolific die-engraver not only of the ancient world, but of all time. There is evidence for his early work at Syracuse about 425 B.C., for work done on behalf of Catana a few years later, then about 413 B.C. dies for Camarina, and a return in 412 B.C. to employment—now annual and regular—at SYRACUSE.

40a. The great deliverance of the city from the menacing Athenian siege gave rise to an annual commemoration known as the Assinarian Games. In the older Greek Games the prizes were wreaths of olive, laurel, parsley, or painted pots. But at Syracuse money prizes seem to have been given—large silver pieces each worth ten drachmas (equalling fifty Sicilian litrae). Euainetos and his staff were the chief suppliers of these between about 412 B.C. and 393 B.C., within which period he turned out at least seventy-two different large dies, twenty-four with chariots and forty-eight with heads of the goddess. These heads vary greatly—not in technical ability—but in artistic quality, and certain dies which carried his signature were not his best. It was at the latter end of this engraver's career that he produced a die with a very pleasing head of the young goddess of Syracuse, framed as usual by four rubber-tough dolphins and having on either side of the neck a little griffin's head, the significance of which escapes us.

41a. Gold coins were not frequently minted in Sicily; but when an emergency arose and ships must be built, or armies equipped, the State's gold reserve was tapped. The ambi-

40 a

tions and conquests of Dionysius, ruler of Syracuse after 405 B.C., were the cause of such an issue as this gold piece—worth one hundred Sicilian litrae, and therefore two of the silver ten-drachma coins—with a fine sophisticated head of the goddess and a little star behind. No room for dolphins here. Euainetos engraved this die.

40 b

Victorious chariots were a standard type for all four-drachma coins of SYRACUSE for a period of close upon two centuries. On those occasions, comparatively rare, when large ten-drachma pieces were minted, chariots were also the rule, for EUAINETOS deliberately followed the lead given in 479 B.C. by the engraver of the Demareteia (No. 15).

41 b

40b. The expert presentation of a chariot by this engraver was already evident about 425 B.C. on the first surviving coin that bears his signature (No. 35), and this skill was unimpaired on the last of all Syracusan dies that can be attributed to him. Action, energy, poise: these in almost perfect equilibrium are shown in the four horses, in their driver, and in the flying Nike above. Then comes a hard ground-line, and below an awkward little assemblage. Reference to 'Prizes' was required by the occasion for which this and similar coins were minted. Therefore, you see from right to left a crested helmet, a greave, cuirass, another greave, a shield side-on, and over it the word ᾽Αθλα, 'prizes'. It looks as though prize suits of armour as well as large handsome coins were given to successful competitors.

41b. Look now at the reverse of the gold coin, so much smaller in size, but intrinsically worth any two of the large silver ten-drachma pieces. A date not so far removed from 395 B.C. must be assigned alike to the larger silver and the smaller gold coin. Anyway, the latter may be nearly fifteen years later than a coin (No. 33) made for Heraclea by Phrygillos. The subject on both is that popular Greek theme—Herakles choking the lion of Nemea. Here, in Syracuse, Euainetos produced not so good a lion, a Herakles of merit equal to the one made by Phrygillos, and a total composition so far superior to the group by Phrygillos, that you can only be astonished at the brilliance even in his later years of the great Euainetos.

AMPHIPOLIS, founded by the Athenians on the banks of the river Strymon between Macedon and Thrace, was a source of trouble to its founders. From the first the colony may have contained a large proportion of men who disliked the growing democratisation of Athens; and there were men of distinguished families, which had long-standing connections with the regions of Thrace, who were perhaps glad to get away from the powerful Demos at home. Thus, when the Spartan Brasidas, in 424 B.C., entered the town, he was received as a 'Liberator', and Amphipolis broke with her mother-city.

42. Somewhere between 415 and 410 B.C. a silver coinage was started which emphasised the break. The other great Athenian colony—Thurii in the west—never gave up the head of Athene as its main type (see No. 26), even when it was no longer friendly to Athens. But Amphipolis took other gods for patrons—Apollo and Artemis. His head, facing upon the coin's obverse, and on its reverse the racing-torch used in the Games held for Artemis, are the witnesses. You have seen the impressive facing head created about 415 B.C. at Catana (No. 38) by Herakleidas. The facing Apollo at Amphipolis is in equal degree a product of Athenian art. It is, indeed, a possibility that this head was the work of KIMON who could have been a member of the anti-democratic Philaïd clan, in which the name was a common one, and such a man would most naturally gravitate to Thrace. Observe that the celator who made this die showed the suggestion of a springing shoulder on one side of the god's neck, a refinement which recurred on Kimon's facing head at Syracuse. Apollo's hair, combed up from his forehead, is pressed forward again

42

lightly by the wreath that rests upon it. From his temple the hair blows out naturally to hide all but the lobe of his ear. The suggestion of sunburnt youth is conveyed both by the surface treatment, and by the subtle gradation of planes.

43

It seems likely that at some time between 410 and 400 B.C. KIMON became a colleague of Euainetos to share the task of producing for SYRACUSE large ten-drachma prize-coins for the Assinarian Games (see No. 40). He also made dies for gold coins which closely resembled those produced by his colleague.

43. The Kimonian prize-coin had on one side a chariot which did not differ greatly from a typical four-horse equipage by the other man, save that the horses were more 'flat out' in their gallop. It is the other side that arrests your attention because the girl-goddess is so different a girl. But first consider some details. Kimon was a little exercised about the right way to finish a neck-truncation, and found it useful to employ one of his four dolphins to modify any hard effect below the neck. On one of his famous dies he set his signature upon the under-neck dolphin, perhaps because its importance was so great to him. His signature K I, and M below these letters, is set on the centre of the hair-band of the girl's forehead; this band, with a fine fringe, appears between her ear and the nape of her neck; but it is knotted on top of her head. She also wears a net which contains her back-hair. Stray locks escape from the forehead and temple to blow back over the silken band. In her ear is a delicate triple-pendant ear-ring, and she wears a necklet of pearls. The goddess by Euainetos (No. 40) had the stiff reeds of some water-plant in her hair, but Kimon's girl has nothing of this kind. Just as the goddess on the first of the Syracusan ten-drachma coins of 479 B.C. (No. 15) seemed portrait-like, so here she seems once more so. Only now you are looking upon the likeness of the sophisticated daughter of some wealthy Syracusan aristocrat.

KIMON made about 410 B.C. two dies, with a head of Arethusa facing, for the people of SYRACUSE. They were for four-drachma coins. One die was not altogether a success: but the other—this one—was the work of genius transfigured by passion. It deserves careful description.

44a. The goddess-nymph, Arethusa, faces you, her hair is wind-blown and confined only by a broad band over the forehead. On the band, as though it was his gift to her, the artist has set his name, *Κιμων*. The eyes are large; the lips full and youthful. Though the left ear is hidden by the hair, you can see part of an ear-ring. Round her neck is a plain circlet and under this a necklace with ten pendant pearls. On the left a dolphin comes diving out of her hair to meet a second whose long snout comes from behind her right shoulder. On the right of the coin are two more plunging dolphins: four dolphins are by now a fixed tradtion for coins of Syracuse. Finally, outside the inner circle which frames the whole, at the very top appears her name, *Αρεθοσα*. There is something here in the quality of the relief, in the fine finish of the truncation, in the bigness of the eyes and in the shape of the cheek and chin that show great resemblance to the silver of Amphipolis (No. 42). If the two coins are not the work of the same artist, at least it can be said that they are akin in their Attic quality and are very closely related. Of some fifteen specimens which have survived from the die, this one alone is almost faultless in its preservation. None the less, much romance has shimmered around this vision of Kimon's Arethusa. There has been poetry, romantic and sentimental, in at least three modern languages: it is wiser to withhold any modern interpretation and to content yourself with admitting that Kimon had good fortune as well as skill in creating one of the world's masterpieces.

44a

44ᵇ

Just as Kimon made two dies with the facing head of Arethusa, so he also made two chariot dies to go with them. Again, one was better than the other, and again you see the more brilliant of the two.

44b. A four-horse chariot is moving to the left, the horses in high action. The nearest horse has strange folds upon its shoulder. The third horse turns its head towards the charioteer, who holds all eight reins in his left hand but adjusts the group of four right-handed reins with his right hand, which also holds a whip. He appears almost too big for the frail basket of the chariot in which he stands, but not as oversized as were some charioteers on earlier coins. Over the horses flies a winged Nike, holding in her out-stretched hands a wreath which she is about to place on the head of the charioteer. Here, in wing, swirling garment and bodily poise, is a very early example of the perfectly-designed flying figure, the prototype of all successful later Greek Nikes, of Victoria in the art of the Roman period, and of all angels in Christian iconography which give an impression of possible flight by beings of human shape. The precise way in which this Nike is adapted to fit the space above the horses can only be called masterly. Under the chariot is a double gound-line and between the two lines the letters $K\iota\mu\omega\nu$ clearly visible. Lower still in a straight line is the name 'of the Syracusans', and under this again an ear of corn. The chariots on the coins of Sicily are mostly able to delight. Dignity is what you are most aware of in those of the Demareteion and the earlier coins of Selinus (Nos. 15, 19). Realism is at its best in those designed by Euainetos and his fellows (Nos. 35, etc.), but for technique and ability in composition, Kimon's chariot, perfectly adjusted to its circle, excels.

Ostentation, strange though this saying may seem, can sometimes achieve great merit, provided the thing shown be grand. The Greek city of AKRAGAS lay on the southerly coast of Sicily, remote from the group of States in the eastern region of the island. From the time of its first coinage the city had shown two blazons, an eagle and a crab, the first upon the obverse, the other upon the reverse of the silver coins. The eagle was perhaps a punning type, for the Doric Greek adjective 'akragas' means 'harsh' or 'strong'—a suitable word to apply to an eagle.

45a. Be that as it may, the keen imagination of Greek celators in the later fifth century soon turned one eagle into two; and when these were shown perched on the body of a dead hare, set upon a rocky peak, many a Greek's thought turned to verses early in the Agamemnon of Aeschylus, where there is described an omen that occurred to Agamemnon and Menelaus. Men saw two eagles, representing the two kings, devouring a pregnant hare. Aloof as the Akragantines were from the other Greeks, they could not fail to be stirred to emulation in the minting of fine coinage, and the names of two celators who set their signatures upon the city's coins are known: POLYKRATES and Myr[on]. The latter seems to have made chariot dies; but it is to the former that the eagles of this great ten-drachma coin should most probably be attributed, at some date very near to 411 B.C. If these large coins were minted mainly with the intention of showing the world that Akragas could strike coins as large as Syracuse could, then ostentation was the motive. The grasshopper in the field behind the birds is out of place and scale, but some mint-

45 a

master's ruling rather than the artist's taste must explain this. Yet the whole design—
one bird that stoops to tear its prey, and one that lifts its head in a shriek of triumph—is
masterly.

45 b

While Polykrates made eagle-dies for AKRAGAS, it seems likely that various chariot-dies—this large one perhaps included—were the work of the other celator, MYR[ON].

45b. A naked god with wind-blown hair, a wisp of scarf around him, drives a four-horse chariot through the air. Over the near horses an eagle with a serpent in its claws flies skyward; a crab drops topsy-turvy earthward, but no ground-line is in sight. The young god, in perfect control of his team, is swinging it round towards you; for his right hand, which holds the four reins that run to the right sides of the horses' mouths, is extended; his left hand is drawn in close to his body and pulls on the left reins so as to bring the horses round. The great city in which this coin was struck was a foundation of Rhodes where the chief deity was Helios, and this is surely the bright sun-god himself driving his chariot through the noon-day sky. Over the horses' heads and under the eagle's wing is the name Ἀκραγας; but this must be a label for the eagle, just as the identical label accompanied the eagle on numerous coins of the city minted a whole century earlier. It cannot name the youth, neither can the youth be a river-god, for such do not drive chariots. The floating scarf and the wind-blown hair are the very attributes of Helios himself. Silver coins of this size are known to have been mounted in drinking-cups, let into the bottoms of their bowls. Pliny—or some other writer whom Pliny cited —apparently saw one of these and, reading the word Ἀκραγας, took it to be the signature of an artist whom he promptly incorporated in his list of celators. Thus Pliny added one more blunder to his comedy of errors. In the year 406 B.C., not long after the production of this great coin, the city of Akragas was captured and destroyed in the brutal Carthaginian invasion.

46 a

Helios appeared in the east about three years after he became a coin-type in the western city of Akragas (No. 45) and, notably enough, in RHODES, the very island from which many centuries before colonists had sailed to found Akragas. In 408 B.C. the three large cities of the island of Rhodes made an agreement to abandon their ancient sites and united to form the single powerful city of Rhodes at the island's northern tip.

46a. Now a new city requires, not a new god, but a new conception of godhead, and the Rhodians created this for Helios, in whose honour the world-famed Colossus was soon to be set up. And the head of Helios henceforward appeared facing as the main coin-type. Most earlier four-drachma pieces and several smaller coins were from dies made by

an artist with powerful imagination and a painterly technique. His individuality is so marked that he must be named the Helios Master, because he invented this radiant sun-god with wind-blown hair. Die-engraving came easily to him, though by profession he was probably a painter.

47a. The region which produced the greatest number of picture-like coins was the island of Crete, and the chief city to employ this style, GORTYNA. Here, on a silver two-drachma coin, made about 380 B.C. or soon after, is the fragment of a strange sacred story now become a fairy-tale. Zeus in the guise of a bull tempted the Princess Europa to mount his back and carried her overseas to Crete. For the moment the bull-god has left her sitting in the broad fork of an ancient willow-tree. Her hair is stiff with brine, her thin clinging raiment wet with spray, her head resting on her left hand suggests sleep and a dream of her lover, who is going to appear soon in the shape of an eagle. The great rough trunk of the tree which she sits upon takes on the vague shape of an eagle's head—as in dreams.

47ª

Rhodes, become a single city, took as its coat-of-arms a punning-type—the Rose.

46b. The thick four-drachma coin of fine silver seems the perfect medium for this amazing picture of still-life. The calyx has opened and the sepals give their stiff support to the soft petals. Easy to think of green and rose-pink here. To the right a young bud, tightly-closed, will soon gain strength. Down by your left hand the little seated sphinx—badge of some mint-master—is like some pottery trifle taken from a shelf to fill the composition. A few letters, Ροδιων, above tell that this is a coin of the Rhodians.

47b. The two-drachma coin of the people of GORTYNA in Crete—inscribed Γορτυνιων below—tells on its reverse here more of the weird story of Europa. Zeus-bull, as you saw, has left his Princess seated in the old willow, to dry her drenched robe and body in the sun, to rest after the long hard ride, and to dream, as he wills her to dream, of an eagle. There is nothing tired about the god with his jaunty tail and sensual tongue and the

47^b

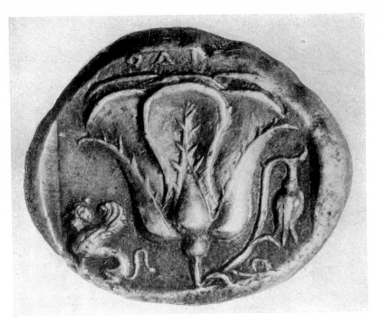

46b

lecherous twinkle in his eye. The people of Gortyna appear to have been so pleased with this story that engravers spread it out over several varied coins, for there were sequels, though made by artists less competent than the man who made the coin you see. There followed one on which Zeus, now in the shape of an eagle, perched upon the tree beside Europa, and Bull, mortal and not indwelt of a god, was startled by a buzzing fly. In a third scene the coin showed the same Bull now maddened by the gad-fly, while on the coin's obverse Bird and Princess were shown united in love. The painterly character of these coins suggests that they were inspired by narrative frescoes on view in Gortyna with the story of Zeus and Europa.

49 a

Dignity was a mark of divinity in most of the ancient world, and it was very rare to find on the money of any State, except for some in Crete, traces of flippant fairy-tales. In Greece itself, and especially in Peloponnesus during the fourth century, the idea of Zeus as Father of all appears to have grown in favour among thoughtful men. Phidias, that most celebrated of all celators, was said to have added something to religion when he made the gold and ivory statue at Olympia. It is certain that he added something to religious art.

48a. In 370 B.C. a large number of Arcadians united to found a federal capital which was named MEGALOPOLIS, and which looked to Zeus as patron of the new city. Two engravers were commissioned to prepare dies and permitted to display abbreviated signatures. Their style shows so strong a family likeness that these men were probably either father and son, or older and younger brothers. It is to the younger man, whose name began with OLYM . . . , that this head of Zeus of about 370 B.C. must be attributed. While the head may owe something to the art of the previous century, it is mainly a product of its own age. Engravers who belonged to what may be called the Olympic tradition, because the finest art of Peloponnesus centred on Olympia, sometimes made dies for Cretan cities.

48 a

49a. Such a tradition is evident in the coins of a city named SYBRITA, in which two gods, Dionysos and Hermes, appear to have had equal honour. The former on the obverse of a thick two-drachma coin—his heavy mass of hair wreathed with ivy, grapes before his face—bears a marked resemblance to Zeus, his father. A date between 370 and 350 B.C. would seem right for this coin, which has the air of a work by the Peloponnesian OLYM . . . who cut dies for the Arcadians, and probably also for a mint in the great Olympian sanctuary itself.

48 b

Both the celators who made the first dies for the new Arcadian city of MEGALOPOLIS produced the same types and set their signatures upon the rock on which a young god is seated. 'Chari . . .', the older man, led the way, but it was the younger, OLYM . . . , who made the finer design.

48b. You have already seen Pan seated upon a rock on a die made about fifty years earlier by Phrygillos in Italy (No. 32). Here in Arcadia the young god is wilder, tougher, with the legs of a runner, full of dangerous energy. Little horns spring from his forehead,

49 b

his right-hand holds a hunter's curved throwing-stick, and below, against the rock, rests his set of Pan-pipes. The monogram in front resolves itself into ARKA, for the Arcadians. 49b. At SYBRITA the reverse of the coin, perhaps attributable to OLYM . . . , presents a head of Hermes. There were tougher representations of both the gods of Sybrita minted elsewhere, and about a century before, for the two gods here are gentle, human-like beings compared with the Great Divinities of Naxos (No. 18) and of Aenus (No. 16). To make gods seem as gentle as this pair in Crete is apt to enfeeble the faith of the people. But this Hermes, with his caduceus held in front of his face, has much charm; and the effect of sunshine and heat is once again suggested, providing a subtle relationship to the first coin of Rhodes (No. 46). Of course, the wide sun-hat, with its ribbon passing round the back of the head, contributes as much as does the far-away look in the eye to this open-air sunniness. The inscription reads Συβριτιων. Because the work of this celator seems of the Olympic tradition, do not think that this in any way separates it from the over-all domination of Attic art. In Peloponnesus, as in the West, you will always find that the finest works are a part of the Athenian tradition which ran from Daidalos to Praxiteles.

You do not really need to know the name of an artist provided you can be made aware of him through his work. Nevertheless, it is more satisfactory to know his name than only part of it; and to know only part of it than to invent for him a label or number. In Peloponnesus you may expect no more than two or three letters of a name, as in the

51

case of the celator PO. . . . He signed some dies in the secondary mint—Hera's mint—at Olympia perhaps in 380 B.C. He made others, four years later I think, for the same mint; and in about 375 B.C. for the island of Zakynthos. In 372 B.C. he made some dies with eagles' heads for the main mint at Olympia, and he is found at work in 370 and 366 B.C. in the Peloponnesian cities of Pheneus and Aigion.

50. It was at PHENEUS that he produced one of his most attractive works, showing the

head of a nymph with blades of iris in her hair, and his signature behind the neck. This nymph is Maia, mother by Zeus of Hermes, whose cult in this city was dominant. Hermes appears carrying the infant Arkas on the coin's reverse.

51. The head of Zeus on an OLYMPIAN two-drachma piece of about 340 B.C. was the

50

work of another and anonymous engraver, who was powerfully under the influence of the Praxitelean Hermes at Olympia. Here is one of several dies by the same man, whom I should have guessed to have been an actual associate of Praxiteles. This is a soft subtle face for the King of the Gods, and, much-praised though it has been, it can never compare with the mighty head (No. 24) made for Olympia some eighty years before. On the coin's reverse is seen an eagle perched on the top of an Ionic capital.

52

There was something unusual and distinctive about the money of CYZICUS, which for about three centuries produced heavy staters of white gold with a type on one side only. You have already seen one such coin (No. 9) of an earlier period with a kneeling Herakles and a tunny-fish, the city's actual coat-of-arms.

52. Here again the same fish is present under the head's truncation and the head itself is an arresting subject: the portrait of an elderly weather-beaten man, nearly bald, and wearing a wreath of laurel. Portraiture on coins and gems began about 440 B.C.—earlier than is usually supposed. This coin should probably be dated to about 350 B.C. when the creation of portrait-heads and statues by celators and bronze-workers was not rare, and some sculptors were even making attempts at it. It is not possible to say who this

53

man may be, but it most likely is an eminent citizen of Cyzicus—an Admiral, perhaps—who wore a signet-ring with his own portrait, and had it reproduced on the coinage when he became for a year Master of the Mint.

53. The second white-gold stater of the same city is something of a contrast because it bears the head of a child. Here is a round-faced little boy, three or four years old, with straggly hair. His neck rests on a nice fat tunny-fish, and a lock of hair curls round the fish's tail. A soft cap of tam-o'-shanter type is on the child's head, and you suddenly realise that this is meant to be a baby-god when you notice in front of his neck the head of his caduceus. This is the child Hermes, the baby trickster of the famous Hymn to Hermes, who from birth was a source of trouble to gods and men.

54 a

Engravers who signed dies normally used their names, or only a few letters of their names, as signatures. But in some rare cases the word ἐποίει, 'made it', was added. Such was the practice of the famous and brilliant THEODOTOS of CLAZOMENAE.

54a and 55a. From about 380 B.C., for some twenty years, this genius made dies for the city, which lay in Ionia not far from Smyrna. His employment coincided with a period of prosperity in the State, for he made dies not only for silver four-drachma pieces, as here, but also for lesser silver coins and for some in gold. Of the two large coins shown only one bears the words Θεοδοτος εποει (*sic*), 'Theodotos made it'; but you observe that the other, with its square jaw, parting of locks, expressive eyes and well-marked brows, is by the same hand. The second coin has suffered much from oxidisation; but so great is the art of this remarkable man, so fine his conception of Apollo, that quality still shines through. Unflagging excellence in Greek art was due to celators and to them alone. Throughout the history of this, as of any other art, lapses in taste occurred. The fourth

century saw a grievous falling-off in vase-painting, the third and later centuries produced a huge load of inferior sculpture; but in celature quality held, for the simple reason that this art constantly employed the most gifted men with standards often as high as those of Theodotos. Consider this problem of a facing head on a coin. You can list seven names of great engravers who made such heads, and many anonymous others. Yet when you meet a coin that has seen much circulation, so that the facing nose is rubbed, you may blame the maker of such a die. Wrongly perhaps; for celators made coins, not only for prolonged circulation in markets, but also for storage in caches, vaults and sanctuaries, whence emerging some day they might rekindle old delights in their fortunate possessors.

55 a

Continents have come strangely by their names: Europe from a girl in a fairy-tale; Asia possibly from a meadow. The Asian meadow of Homer, by the banks of Cayster near Ephesus, abounded in wild fowl, and thirty miles further north were more streams and meadows to make a paradise for water-birds near the city of CLAZOMENAE. This name suggested the Greek word κλάζω, meaning clash or whirr, screech or cry—often used of the noise made by the wings or voices of wild fowl, for which reason the men of Clazomenae took the swan as the punning-badge for their city. Moreover, the bird was sacred to Apollo, whose head was on the other side of their coins.

55 *b*

54ᵇ

54b and 55b. These magnificent birds are assuredly the work of THEODOTOS. The inscriptions run: *Κλαζομενιον* and *Κλαζο*, along with the names of magistrates named Metrodoros and Mandronax—details which you forget in the presence of these mighty swans. One with his beak preens the big pinions inside his raised left wing; the other, wings up, advances bold and wild. I have heard swans called ungainly out of water: Theodotos knew differently. Observe the recession in depth of the far wings; note the exquisite art of the feathering such as calls for comparison with the art of Dexamenos, gem-engraver of Chios sixty years earlier, who loved cranes as much as Theodotos loved swans. He was probably an Athenian for he does not spell in an Ionian fashion, and during the fourth century numerous celators and sculptors from Athens were being employed in Asia Minor. Perhaps his thought turned to the second book of the *Iliad*: 'And as the many tribes of feathered birds, wild geese or cranes or long-necked swans, on the Asian meadow by Cayster's stream, fly hither and thither delighting in their plumage, and with loud cries settle ever onwards, and the meadow resounds; even so poured forth the many tribes of warriors from ships and tents into the Scamandrian plain.'

A SHORT LIST OF RECENT BOOKS
WITH SOME ENLARGEMENTS OF GREEK COINS

H. A. CAHN, *Die Münzen der sizilischen Stadt Naxos*, Bâle, 1944.

A. GALLATIN, *The Syracusan Decadrachms of the Euainetos Type*, Harvard, 1930.

G. F. HILL, *Select Greek Coins*, Vanoest, Paris, 1927.

G. F. HILL, *Guide to the Principal Coins of the Greeks*, British Museum, London, 1932.

O. RAVEL, *Les Poulains de Corinthe*, Bâle, 1936.

E. RIZZO, *Monete Greche della Sicilia*, Rome, 1946.

C. SELTMAN, *Greek Coins*, Methuen, London, 1933.

C. SELTMAN, *Approach to Greek Art*, Studio, London, 1948.

NOTES ON THE ESSAY

a. To page 8: on the temple of Artemis at Ephesus, note that E. Löwy (in 'Sitzungs Berichte der Akademie der Wissenschaften in Wien'; Phil. hist. Kl., *CCXII, 4; 1932) endeavoured to overthrow the conclusions of Hogarth and to make out the foundation-deposit—coins and ivories and all—to be a whole century later. It seems strange that he did not know of the Spartan excavations of 1906 to 1910, which totally support Hogarth's dating. Löwy does not mention them.*

b. To page 9: concerning the attitude of the Greeks to artists, see my Approach to Greek Art, *pp. 12 f., 69, 76 ff.*

c. To page 10: on the Pythagorean system and early coins of Magna Graecia, see especially G. F. Hill, Historical Greek Coins, *1906, pp. 23 ff.; E. Babelon,* Traité des Monnaies gr., *Part ii, Vol. i, 1373 ff.; Charles Seltman,* Greek Coins, *pp. 77 ff.*

d. To page 13: for a short description of the Greek method of coining money see Seltman, op. cit., pp. 20 ff.

e. To page 14: AR . . . the earliest signature: see E. Boehringer, Münzen von Syrakus, *1929, p. 80. Accordingly, 'Euth . . .', whose signature I formerly (op. cit., p. 107) described as 'the earliest', is now to be called the second earliest.*

f. To page 15: The Master of Olympia as an expert in wood-carving; see my Approach to Greek Art, *p. 62 f.*

g. To page 15: for the picture, on the fragment of a cup by Duris, of a youth holding a bowl with central boss, see J. C. Hoppin, Handbook of Attic R.F. Vases, *1919, Vol. i, p. 253.*

h. To page 16: Aristophanes goes to considerable trouble to attack well-known people in 'The Birds', notably 'Phrygilos', line 763, and 'Exekestides', line 764.

i. To page 17: Sosion and Eumenes, neither very good; see L. Tudeer, Tetradrachmenprägung von Syrakus in der Periode der signierenden Künstler, *Berlin 1913, pp. 217 ff.*

k. To page 17: Prokles of Naxos; see my review of H. A. Cahn, 'Die Münzen der sizilischen Stadt Naxos', *1944, in* Classical Review, *1946, p. 118.*

l. To page 18: the work of Eukleidas, see L. Tudeer, op. cit., and Seltman, Greek Coins, *p. 126.*

m. To page 18: the lead 'pattern' for a decadrachm in the manner of Phrygillos is in the collection of Professor A. B. Cook.

n. To page 19: the celator Kimon is mentioned by Athenaeus, XI, 781 e.

o. To page 20: eyesight of engravers; A. Gallatin, Dekadr. Euainetos, *thought engravers strained their eyes: but see Aristoph.,* Clouds, *766 ff., for a rock crystal lens in use in 423 B.C.*

p. To page 22: for a general account of the money of Alexander and his successors, see Seltman, Greek Coins, *Chapters XII to XIV.*

NOTES ON THE DESCRIPTIONS

Every coin is shown in its Actual Size (A.S. in the following list) and one or both sides are shown as Enlargements (E.) the dimensions of which vary from about three diameters to four diameters—once six diameters. The coins on any one page are always enlarged in the same proportion. If one specimen is used for A.S. but a different one for E., this is noted in the list. The great majority of the pictures are photographs of the original coins, but in a few cases of fine electrotype facsimiles. Weights in an essay on coins as works of art are irrelevant; therefore omitted. The coins are of silver unless otherwise stated.

1. ELECTRUM: Lion's head. *British Museum.*

2. ELECTRUM: Goat. *Brit. Mus.*

3. AEGINA, DIDRACHM: Turtle. *Charles Seltman.*

4. ACANTHUS, TETRADRACHM: Lioness on bull. *Brit. Mus.*

5. ATHENS, PEISISTRATUS, TETRADRACHM: Athene/Owl. *E. G. Spencer-Churchill.* Dating to 566 B.C., see my paper in *Numismatic Chronicle*, 1946, pp. 97 ff.

6. ATHENS, HIPPIAS, TETRADRACHM: Athene/Owl. *Brit. Mus.*

7. METAPONTUM, DIDRACHM: Barley. *Brit. Mus.*

8. POSEIDONIA, DIDRACHM: Poseidon. *Brit. Mus.*
   There is a famous representation of a primitive statue on a hydria in Naples by Epiktetos II (= Kleophrades painter), *ca.* 510–480 B.C. The coin of Poseidonia gives a somewhat earlier picture of a statue which was already old when the coin-die was made.

9. CYZICUS, ELECTRUM: Herakles. *Brit. Mus.*

10. PEPARETHOS, TETRADRACHM: Grapes/Winged god. *Brit. Mus.*

11. ATHENS, DECADRACHM: Athene/Owl. *Berlin.*
    On the annual bonus see my *Greek Coins*, pp. 92 ff.

12. AENUS, TETRADRACHM: Hermes/Caduceus. *R. C. Lockett.*

13. SIPHNOS, DIDRACHM: Apollo/Falcon. *Paris.*

14. LYCIA, DIDRACHM: Aphrodite/Tetraskeles. *Brit. Mus.*
    The curious reverse design is discussed by A. B. Cook, *Zeus*, i, pp. 299 ff., who regards it as the symbol of Kyklops, son of Ouranos. But Aphrodite was the daughter of Ouranos (= Uranus); therefore she too has a claim to this symbolic solar wheel.

15. SYRACUSE, DECADRACHM 'DEMARETEION': Chariot/Goddess. *Brit. Mus.*
On AR . . . see note (*e*) above.

16. AENUS, TETRADRACHM: Hermes/Goat and Throne. *Boston Mus. Fine Arts.*
On Hermes as protector, and his concern with flocks see Jacqueline Chittenden, 'The Master of Animals', in *Hesperia*, 16, 1947, pp. 89 ff.

17. AETNA, TETRADRACHM: Seilenos/Zeus. *Brussels.*

18. NAXOS, TETRADRACHM: Dionysos/Seilenos. *Brit. Mus.*
For Anakles see my *Approach to Greek Art*, Pl. 56*b*.

19. SELINUS, TETRADRACHM: Chariot/Young god. *R. C. Lockett.*

20. SELINUS, DIDRACHM: Herakles/Young god. *R. C. Lockett.*

21. TROIZEN, DRACHM: Athene/Trident. *Charles Seltman.*

22. MYTILENE, ELECTRUM: Apollo. *Brit. Mus.*

23. AMBRACIA, STATER: Pegasus/Athene. *Brit. Mus.*

24. OLYMPIA, DIDRACHM: Zeus/Thunderbolt. *Berlin.*

25. OLYMPIA, DIDRACHM: Eagle/Thunderbolt. *Boston.* Frontispiece: (*formerly*) *Woodward.*

26. THURII, DIDRACHM: Athene/Bull. *Brit. Mus.*

27. TERINA, DIDRACHM: Nike/Nike. *Brit. Mus.*
On the work in various cities of the engraver of this and 26 and 32, see G. F. Hill, *Guide to the Principal Coins of the Greeks*, 1932, p. 25, nos. 21f.

28. HYELE, DIDRACHM: Lion/Nymph. *Brit. Mus.* (*Lloyd Coll.*).

29. LEONTINI, TETRADRACHM: Apollo/Lion-waterspout. *Boston.*

30. SYRACUSE, TETRADRACHM: Chariot/Goddess. *A.S. R. C. Lockett; E. chariot Paris; E. goddess Lockett.*

31. SYRACUSE, TETRADRACHM: Chariot/goddess. *A.S. R. C. Lockett; E. chariot Paris; E. goddess Lockett.*
For the New York bowl with similar chariots, see G. M. A. Richter, *Amer. Journ. Arch.*, 45, 1941, pp. 363 ff.

32. PANDOSIA, DIDRACHM: Hera/Pan. *Boston.*

33. HERACLEA, DIDRACHM: Athene/Herakles. *Brit. Mus.*

34. SINOPE, DRACHM: Nymph/Sea-eagle. *R. C. Lockett.*

35. SYRACUSE, TETRADRACHM: Chariot/Goddess. *Lloyd and Brit. Mus.*

36. CATANA, TETRADRACHM: Chariot/Young god. *Berlin.*

37. CATANA, DRACHM: Chariot/Young god. *Penisi Collection.*
    This is enlarged to six diameters.

38. CATANA, TETRADRACHM: Apollo/Chariot. *A.S. Penisi and Brit. Mus.; E. Penisi.*

39. CAMARINA, TETRADRACHM: Chariot/Herakles. *A.S. Brit. Mus. and Naples; E. Naples.*
    There is a unique coin with the engraver's signature on a tablet in front of the Hero's face in the Jameson Collection, Paris.

40. SYRACUSE, DECADRACHM: Goddess/Chariot. *Penisi and Brit. Mus.*

41. SYRACUSE, GOLD: Goddess/Herakles. *E. G. Spencer-Churchill.*

42. AMPHIPOLIS, TETRADRACHM: Apollo/Race-torch. *Paris.*

43. SYRACUSE, DECADRACHM: Goddess/Chariot. *A.S. Penisi and Brit. Mus.; E. Penisi.*

44. SYRACUSE, TETRADRACHM: Arethusa/Chariot. *Penisi.*

45. AKRAGAS, DECADRACHM: Eagles/Helios. *Munich. Photos Prof. M. Hirmer.*

46. RHODES, TETRADRACHM: Helios/Rose. *Brit. Mus.*

47. GORTYNA, DIDRACHM: Europa/Bull. *Brit. Mus.*

48. MEGALOPOLIS, DIDRACHM: Zeus/Pan. *Brit. Mus. and (formerly) Woodward.*

49. SYBRITA, DIDRACHM: Dionysos/Hermes. *Brit. Mus.*

50. PHENEUS, DIDRACHM: Maia/Hermes. *Brit. Mus.*
    The list of dies by PO . . . is as follows: 380 B.C. Olympia Hera Mint (Seltman, *Temple Coins*, nos. 290 to 292); 376 B.C. Same Mint (*op. cit.*, nos. 293 to 296); 375 B.C. Zakynthos (*Brit. Mus. Cat. Peloponnesus*, p. 96, nos. 24, 25); 372 B.C. Olympia Zeus Mint (Seltman, *op. cit.*, no. 161, and Plate VIII, 19, 20, 22); 370 B.C. this coin of Pheneus; and finally 366 B.C. Aigion (Seltman, *Greek Coins*, Pl. XXXV, 15).

51. OLYMPIA, DIDRACHM: Zeus/Eagle. *Berlin.*
    On the engraver, see my paper in *Hesperia*, 1948, pp. 71 ff.

52. CYZICUS, ELECTRUM: Portrait. *Boston.*

53. CYZICUS, ELECTRUM: Child-Hermes. *Boston.*

54. CLAZOMENAE, TETRADRACHM: Apollo/Swan. *Paris.*

55. CLAZOMENAE, TETRADRACHM: Apollo/Swan. *Paris.*
    A record of forth-century celators and sculptors who went to work in Asia Minor deserves notice. Best known are the following who about 350 B.C. provided designs for, or worked on the Mausoleum: 1. Scopas of Paros, architect, bronze-worker and marble-carver (also worked on Artemision at Ephesus); 2. Bryaxis, an Athenian who also worked in Rhodes, Cnidos and Lycia, and later made an Apollo of wood, gold and marble; 3. Timotheos, as far as is known, only a marble-worker; 4. Leochares of

Athens, a celator who made several gold and ivory figures at Olympia and bronze portraits; he constructed at Halicarnassus a figure of wood and marble, or wood and ivory.

Some of these may have been as artists the equals of Theodotos—none better.

INDEX